SittingAround:
The Complete Guide to Starting Your Own Babysitting Coop

Erica Zidel
Founder, SittingAround.com

Copyright © 2011 by Erica Zidel and SittingAround

All rights reserved. This book or any portion thereof may not be reproduced or used in any manner whatsoever without the express written permission of the publisher except for the use of brief quotations in a book review.
ISBN 978-0-9830229-2-3

INTRODUCTION 4

WHAT A BABYSITTING COOP IS AND WHY YOU
SHOULD JOIN ONE 8

CREATING A COOP 20

RECRUITING MEMBERS 35

YOUR COOP IN ACTION 52

FORMS AND DOCUMENTATION 65

COMMONLY ASKED QUESTIONS 69

APPENDIX 76

Introduction

I decided to write this book because I am the mother of a young child. As a professional, I work hard at my job. As a parent, I work even harder at home. Sometimes (okay, fairly often), I just need a break. I understand all too well the balance most parents try to strike between parting with their hard-earned money for a sitter and parting with their sanity when they don't get those precious moments of quietude. (In fact, as I am writing this preface, my four year old son is flinging stuffed animals down the stairs in a dramatic protest against bedtime.)

The purpose of this book is to introduce you to the concept and benefits of babysitting cooperatives (aka "coops"), a fantastic alternative to pricey sitters that wind up being more fun for kids while building community amongst the parents who participate. I didn't find out about babysitting coops until my son was a toddler, but once I did, I wanted to shout about them from the rooftops and share the benefits with every parent I could find.

Babysitting coops are not widely used in the United States today, and I wanted to know why. I soon discovered that most parents were similar to me in that they had either not heard of babysitting coops or did not know much about them. In fact, when asked about their level of familiarity with babysitting coops, over three-quarters of parents (78%) in a recent survey[1] said they had either

---

[1] Zidel, Erica. "Trends in Babysitting." Survey. 30 August 2010. <https://sittingaround.com/media/blog/SittingAround-Trends-in-Babysitting-

never heard of them or had heard of them, but didn't know much about them. However, when asked in that same survey, "If you could get free babysitting by trading sitting services with other trusted adults, would you?" two-thirds of parents (67%) said yes!

The story here is that we have an education problem: parents would love to participate in babysitting coops if only they knew what they were and how to run one. My goal is to solve that problem by acquainting you with babysitting coops and by providing constructive advice to help you start your own.

The coop that I joined is fantastic – it consists of 25 or so families who live within one mile of my house. Everything about my coop is wonderful except for one thing: my coop is run entirely offline. Records are kept manually, and member lists and rules are distributed via hard copy. Worse yet, anytime a sit takes place, someone needs to inform the secretary, who will in turn record the sit by hand (in what can only be described as the largest 3 –ring binder known to man).

Dreading the day that it would be my turn to manage said binder, I searched and searched for a website that would do the coop management for us – a site that would keep track of our information, the parents who were in our coop, and the transactions that took place between us. After all, the internet is an integral part of my life. I send multiple emails every hour and manage my schedule with an online calendar. I needed a coop website

2010.pdf>

that would fit with my connected lifestyle. Unfortunately, there were few options available online. The few that *did* exist online had clunky interfaces and had been developed by people out of touch with the way our new generation of parents operate. One site, which shall remain nameless, even advocated scheduling sitting using a "phone tree."

Since there was no website that met my needs, I decided the best thing to do was to create the solution myself. I interviewed other parents, developed a feature set, and went to work building the solution I wished that I had when I was starting my search. This tool is now called SittingAround, and can be found at www.sittingaround.com.

This book recommends using SittingAround to manage your babysitting coop, as I built it to fulfill with the very purpose of automating coop management and making life easier for the parents who used it. There are other sites out there that do some of what SittingAround accomplishes; however, I do think SittingAround is the easiest and most feature rich site available to coops today, and so it is the site I recommend using throughout this book.

It is my desire that life be more manageable, more enjoyable, and, of course, more affordable for parents everywhere. I hope that you use this book to learn about babysitting coops, to get inspired to create your own, and to inspire others to participate along with you. The old saying "It takes a village to raise a child" may be clichéd, but it is built upon a fundamental truth: a supported parent is a successful parent. The reality of life in today's modern world means that we no longer live in villages, surrounded by extended family and a network of friends; however, with a little bit of effort and a lot of passion, it is very possible to build your own supportive community to make the trials and tribulations of being a parent a little easier.

Erica Zidel

October, 2011

What a Babysitting Coop is and Why You Should Join One

Those Pricey Little Bundles of Joy

Any way you look at it, raising a child is one of the most expensive things you'll ever do. For a middle-class family, the expected cost of raising a child born in 2010 to age 18 is $286,050 – over a quarter of a million dollars[2]. And this is before you factor in any higher education contributions. Since 1960, child-rearing costs have risen 22 percent in real-terms (i.e. after adjusting for inflation).

      Much of this increased child-rearing cost is due to our growing consumption of childcare. According to the United States Department of Agriculture (USDA), "In 1960, child care costs were negligible, mainly consisting of in-the-home babysitting." In 1960, childcare comprised just 2 percent of the overall childrearing cost. By 2009, that number had jumped to a whopping 17 percent. The average middle-class family in 2009 spent $2,570 on childcare alone (including daycare expenses).

---

[2] For families with HH income between $57,670 and $98,120. Lino, Mark. *Expenditures on Children by Families 2009.* USDA. June 2010.

Babysitting Adds Up Fast

In 2009, the average babysitter in the United States received $10 per hour[3]. The closer you move to major metropolitan areas, the higher that rate goes. In fact, when my son was just six months old (in 2006), I placed an ad on Craigslist, looking for a sitter. At the time, I had no compass for babysitting rates. The last time I had any idea what babysitters made was when I was a sitter myself, as a teen earning $3 per hour for watching three young kids.

My ad specifically said that I needed someone to watch my son at night, after he was asleep. No feedings, no entertaining, and no diapers. The job was pretty cushy. After all, we had high-speed internet and dozens of on-demand movie channels. The sitter would be spending most of the night surfing the web, watching new releases, and snacking on my food while simply keeping an ear out for the errant cry. In the email, I asked the applicants to provide their standard rates.

I was stunned when the first email I received was from a 14 year old girl who told me that her rate was $15 per hour - *minimum*. I honestly thought her email was a joke until similar ones started trickling in. Finally, after a swath of high-schoolers demanding a rate that rivaled my professional salary, I found a responsible 22 year-old who told me she understood that "different families could afford different rates" and agreed to watch our cable (and our son) for a mere $10 per hour.

[3] Genevieve Thiers, "What to Pay a Babysitter," Momlogic. 1 May 2009 <http://www.momlogic.com/2009/05/what_to_pay_your_babysitter.php>

No matter how you slice it, hiring a sitter will significantly increase the cost of a night out or an afternoon of errands. It doesn't matter if you spend $5, $10, or $15 per hour; babysitting adds up fast. I used to wonder where all my money was going until I stopped to realize that the occasional dinner and movie was costing me an average of $65 per night on top of what I was paying for the dinner and movie itself.

There were other drawbacks to my sitter situation as well. While the sitter I selected was older, more settled, and demonstrably more responsible than her younger counterparts, she was still a bit uncomfortable and unnatural with my son. As good as she was, she had no significant experience with young kids - she hadn't learned to distinguish the hungry cry from the tired cry from the wet diaper cry. Plus, her availability varied a lot. She was often around on Saturday nights, but during the day she usually had plans. And, while she tried hard to accommodate last minute requests, I still often found myself passing up invitations and forgoing childcare when I seemed to need it most. Scheduling sits was stressful, not to mention expensive, but it was what I did for the first three years of my son's life.

And then I found a better way.

Babysitting Coops

A babysitting cooperative (aka a "coop") is a group of families who agree to take turns babysitting each other's children. Instead of paying with money, families pay in the form of points. The care-giving family is credited the points for sitting and the care-receiving family is debited the points. The care-giving family, who are members of the coop as well, spend the points they earn to have other families in the group watch *their* children.

The concept of shared childrearing has been around for thousands of years. It used to be that people lived in groups, surrounded by relatives who shared the work of everyday life, childcare certainly notwithstanding. While there were no structured coops back then, there was a strong understanding of reciprocity (everyone pitched in) and there was little worry about the quality of care - children were looked after by experienced and loving relatives.

As people in the developed world eventually stopped living in small family groups (for the most part), childrearing became less and less a shared activity. This shift became particularly pronounced during the mid-1900s. By most accounts, traditional babysitting coops (as we think of them today) sprung up in the late 1940s with the post-war baby boomers. Middle class couples moved to the suburbs en masse and began to find themselves increasingly separated from extended family. Instead, they were surrounded by other young families very similar to themselves. Traditional gender roles solidified, with men traveling to the city for work and women staying at home to raise the children. Mothers, who lacked the support they once had from other female relatives, were now faced with the task of child rearing largely on their own. In response to this problem, it was not long before women came together and formed organized support networks to help one another raise children. Thus, the first babysitting coops were born.

Today, we find ourselves in a rapidly changing world. Families are more spread out than ever before and social networks are constantly in flux. The grandmother who once looked after her grandkids may now visit with them via a webcam instead. Yet while the environment in which we live has changed, the need for a trusted support network has not. If anything, the nomadic nature of our society today makes it that much more critical that we proactively develop our own communities. Add to that childcare costs that continue to rise at a rapid rate despite a trying economic climate, and it is no surprise that babysitting coops are sprouting up across the nation.

Unlike their predecessors from the forties, babysitting coops today take many forms. They may be large groups with structured rules and a well-designed point system; conversely, they may be casual arrangements where neighbors simply call each other up when they need a little extra help. The key is finding – or creating! – the right type of coop to fit your personal needs.

Coop Benefits

Babysitting coops provide a plethora of benefit to their members. In fact, most families who join an active coop find it hard to imagine their life without it. And it's not just the parents who receive value from coops – children profit in many ways, too! Below, just some of the many benefits coops provide.

Save Money. Without question, coops make good financial sense. One of the top reasons parents cite for joining a coop is saving money. Consider this: a family who uses their hired babysitter just twice a month will spend approximately $1200 on babysitting for the year. (Cost varies, since babysitting rates are dependent upon where you live.) Many families, in fact, spend far more than this each year. By contrast, a babysitting coop charges you $0 when you need a sitter – no matter if you need someone for one hour or for the entire day. You pay your sitters in points, points that you accrue by sitting for other member's children. And, as you will quickly realize, sitting for others is quite easy and hardly ever burdensome.

Most coops charge an annual membership fee to cover the cost of group meetings, materials, online coop management, etc. Membership fees typically range from $10 - $50 per year. Even at $50, a coop is still a phenomenal deal. At less than the cost of one night's worth of babysitting, the coop has already paid for itself after the very first time you've used it.

Get High-Quality Childcare. You'd be hard-pressed to find a teenage sitter who provides better childcare than does another parent. Without question, there are some really good, high-quality babysitters out there. However, how many of them can instantly distinguish a hungry cry from a tired cry? How many know the quickest way to diffuse a toddler tantrum? With a hired sitter, you need to interview them and determine whether they *could* do the job; with another parent, they *have* been doing the job.

The numbers bear this out. When asked in a recent survey[4] how satisfied they were with the quality of child care they received, parents were almost twice as likely to say "Extremely Satisfied" with their free babysitters (67%) as with their paid babysitters (38%).

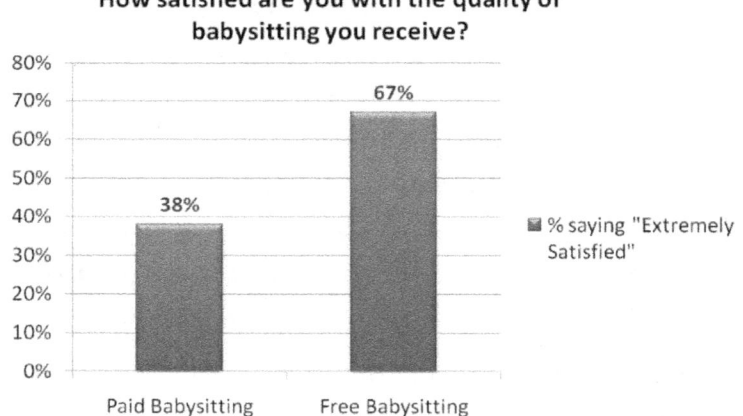

---

[4] Zidel, Erica. "Trends in Babysitting." Survey. 30 August 2010. <https://sittingaround.com/media/blog/SittingAround-Trends-in-Babysitting-2010.pdf>

And, not surprisingly, nearly all (92%) of this free babysitting came from family and/or friends. By contrast, more of the paid babysitting (43%) came from non-related teenagers than from any place else. Explains one mom, "Other moms watch my kids, then I'll watch theirs when they need someone. That's fun for my kids, and I know they're well cared for."

Provide Fun for the Kids. Many parents say that sitting for another family actually makes things easier on them, since sitting for another family gets their children a built-in play date. I am the parent of any only child, and most weekends, the only thing my son wants to do is play. Without any siblings, he turns to me and his father, insisting we participate in an endless loop of Thomas the Train, puzzles, books, and art projects. Don't get me wrong – I love spending time with my son. But when I am trying to make dinner or finish up some work I brought home from the office, it helps to have a friend to entertain him. Plus, let's be honest: try as I might, I'm nowhere near as fun as another child.

By participating in a coop, your children have the opportunity to make new friends and enhance their social development. This is especially true for children without siblings and for those who don't attend daycare or school. Children interact with adults differently than they do with their peers, and it is important that they have the opportunity to develop critical social skills such as sharing and cooperation. Playing with the other kids in the coop is an easy and fun way for them to develop these skills.

Find a Sitter When You Need One. Having many possible sitters means there is almost always someone available when you need them. With hired babysitters, there is the pressure to "use or lose" them - if you don't hire them frequently enough, these sitters may take jobs with other families (and thus not be available when needed). Even if you do have a regular babysitter, remember that this sitter has a life outside of babysitting and it is far from guaranteed that she will be available any time you need her.

By contrast, with a coop, there is almost always another parent available to sit when you need them – be it once a week or once every few months. Think about it – if you are in a coop with ten other parents, you have ten possible sitters at any given time. The chance that one of them will be available when you need a sit is ten times higher than it is for a single babysitter. And the likelihood of finding an available sitter only increases as the size of your coop grows.

Increase Connection to Your Community. By participating in a coop, you'll get to know other parents in your community and you'll interact with them on a frequent basis. A coop doesn't just provide babysitting for your kids – it also provides a strong social network of parents who live nearby and have children close in age to yours. Attending monthly playgroups together and swapping sits helps parents forge new and stronger friendships.

This benefit is especially appreciated by families that are new to a community and / or without a network of extended family nearby. Joining a coop is a great way to meet other parents and recreate the support network you left behind. You may very well find yourself connecting so well with the other members that you end up getting together with them for coffee or dinner as often as you are using them as sitters.

Decrease Dependence on Family and Friends for "Favors." Is grudging grandma your default sitter? Does asking friends to watch your kids leave you feeling guilty? Swapping sitting within a group eliminates the "IOU" effect. Parents don't need to worry about whether it is their turn to sit for someone else or whether they are putting a friend on the spot. In a babysitting coop, sitting is not a favor. It is a transaction between members of the coop, where families receive payment for the services they provide. Families volunteer to sit if they are available and, in exchange for sitting, receive compensation in the form of credits.

Ways to Use the Coop

When I would hire a babysitter, I always wanted to make sure I was getting my money's worth. I would weigh the importance of the event in my mind against the anticipated cost of hiring a sitter. (Did a housewarming party warrant $50 in babysitting cost? Was dinner and a movie worth an extra $70?) As a result, every time I did hire a sitter, I felt pressure to have a really, really good time and make my sitting costs "worth it." Not surprisingly, all of that added pressure actually detracted from my ability to enjoy myself.

A babysitting coop, by contrast, is very freeing in that it is just as easy to use it for a big night out as it is for a few hours of relaxation at a coffee shop. In fact, many parents say that the ease with which they can get some casual time to themselves – and not feel guilty about it! – is one of the best things about being part of a coop. You could easily schedule recurring sittings for the same time each week, giving yourself a break to look forward to. Or, you could schedule sittings on short notice whenever you feel yourself getting run down and needing some time to rejuvenate.

Parents use their coops when they want or need to:

- Run errands
- Go to the gym or take a quiet walk

- Get work done, either at the office or around the house
- Have a night out with their spouse or partner
- Get together with friends
- Read a book
- Take a nap
- Do just about anything else!

Parenting is a demanding job. Whether you work full-time or you are a stay at home parent (or any combination thereof!), you undoubtedly have moments where all you want is a break. Even if that break means doing laundry in a quiet house or grocery shopping without little fingers pulling everything off the shelves. A lot of parents feel guilty about wanting or asking for these breaks, but you shouldn't. With a babysitting coop, everything is reciprocal. One parent gives you a break; you give a break to another. A babysitting coop is like a highly dependable extended network that is ready and willing to help you out whenever you need it.

Creating a Coop

Before you decide to create your own coop, I'd recommend that you first do some research to see if one exists in your area already. You can do this by visiting SittingAround (www.sittingaround.com) and typing in your zip code – the site will let you know if there is already a babysitting coop in your community. If there is, look into joining it. More likely than not, that will be the easiest solution for you. If your search doesn't turn up any nearby coops – or any that you'd want to join – don't fret. Creating a coop is easy to do, especially if you follow the tips laid out here.

To Web or Not to Web?

The very first decision you will need to make is whether or not you will manage your coop using an online coop tool. I would strongly advise you to consider using one of these tools, as they are designed specifically to help simplify coop operations. Translation: They will make your life much, much easier.

Prior to the proliferation of the Internet, coops were run in a very manual way. Typically, coop members would take turns being the coop secretary (each filling the role for a number of months at a time). When parents needed a sitter, they would call the coop secretary. The secretary would then go down the list of members, calling each one until he/she was able to find another family who could fulfill the sitting request. Then, the secretary would call the requesting member to inform him or her that a sitter had been found. Upon completion of the sitting, the secretary would deduct the appropriate number of points from the requesting member (maintained on an Excel spreadsheet) and credit them to the fulfilling member. Exhausted just reading that? Me too.

Thankfully, there are many tools available that reduce the amount of manual tasks required and allow you to perform some to all of your coop's functions online. Whether you choose to use a site designed specifically for babysitting coops or not, the internet will likely be a part of how you run your coop. However, if you anticipate that your coop will include members who are not computer-savvy or who may not have regular access to the Internet, you may want to consider managing your coop entirely offline (this assumes no internet tools whatsoever, including email). Because most people will use the internet to some degree, I won't spend a lot of time in this book discussing completely offline coop management.

Assuming you will use the internet to help run your coop, you will need to decide if a coop management site or a "do-it-yourself" approach is the right solution for your group. In most cases, it is better to use one of the specific coop management sites than to try to create your own process using an amalgamation of non-specific tools. However, each group has unique needs and preferences and the type that a coop selects will ultimately depends upon those needs and preferences of its members.

In most cases, I strongly advocate using a coop management site such as SittingAround (www.sittingaround.com). These sites negate the need for a secretary entirely, as they allow members to create postings when they need a sitter. The postings are then listed on the group's private coop page. Additionally, members can elect to receive email notifications letting them know when a new sit has been requested by a member of their group. Sits are scheduled via the site, which even maintains member profiles and emergency contact information. The site calculates points for sits, transfers them automatically, and maintains a historical record of all sits that have been completed. In fact, just about all coop activity (except, of course, your meetings!) can be managed here. These sites generally charge a small fee – about $20 per member per year. For most people, the coop site membership fee pays for itself after the very first sit.

A quick comparison of the two options below:

Coop Site vs. Do-It-Yourself

	Coop Site	Do-It-Yourself
Cost	Small fee	Generally free
Ease of Use	Easy to use	Requires multiple tools and many workarounds

Time Required of its Members	Low	Moderate
Privacy / Security	High	Moderate - Low

Important! If you decide to use a coop management site, be sure to create an account and register your coop there before conducting any meetings or reaching out to new members.

Find Friends

Although you can definitely start a coop on your own, having a core group of members at the beginning will make it easier. Getting a second member involved will allow you to divide up the work of setting up the coop and have someone to bounce ideas off. Getting a third member involved will allow you to get your coop up and running right away, since three members are all you need to start swapping babysitting. Additionally, the other members can be a big help by referring prospective members and enabling the coop to grow organically.

Once you have a core group of founding members – three to four is best – schedule a preliminary meeting. During this meeting, you and the other founding members must make important decisions about how you want to operate your coop. While this book highlights the topics you should discuss (at a minimum) and makes recommendations, it is really up to you to create the kind of coop you want.

Name Your Coop

Although it's straightforward, naming your coop is something you should spend a few moments thinking about. Make sure you give your coop a name that is meaningful to both its members and to those who might become members in the future. Most coops serve a general geographic area or an organization, and they should communicate that in their name. If your coop is for families whose children attend East Elementary school, you would be well-served to simply call it the "East Elementary Babysitting Coop."

A word of caution in naming your coop: don't be too vague or broad. If you live in a big city like New York, you should avoid using a name such as "New York City Parents Coop." Unless you're targeting parents across the entirety of the city, you should use a more specific name – for example, "Lower East Side NYC Coop." In big cities, it often helps if you use the name of a neighborhood or even a zip code.

Set Geographic Boundaries

Before your coop is up and running, you should decide what the geographic boundaries of your coop will be. The geographic boundaries are the areas within which all coop members must reside. Even if you plan to be flexible with the boundaries, it is a good idea to set them up so that members understand how far they may be expected to travel for it a sit.

The easiest way to set boundaries is to pull up a map of your neighborhood, town, or city (depending on how large you want the geographic area to be). Choose a north, south, east, and west limit for the coop. Or, if that is too specific for you, choose an area (e.g. the Fremont neighborhood). As you select these limits, consider how far you'd be comfortable traveling, as well as how large you expect the coop to be. Generally, the more members you'd like to have in your coop, the greater the geographic area you should span. Document the limits so that you can communicate them to members and prospects in the future.

Determine How to Admit Members

It is important to determine upfront what the process for admitting members will be. How does a prospective member apply to join? Who can approve or deny a prospective member? There are a number of specific questions you will need to consider:

- What qualifications must a prospect have? Qualifications you may consider include:

    o *Living in a specific area* – You don't want members having to travel long distances in order to get a sitter. Does the prospect live within the boundaries you defined? Prospects who are on the border may be considered on a case-by-case basis

    o *Attending a certain school* – Some coops prefer to base qualification for membership on attending the same school or community organization. Doing this makes it more likely that everyone in the coop will know each other well, especially the children (many of whom will already be friends)

    o *Having children of a similar age* – A lot of times, coops will try to ensure that the children in the group are relatively close in age. This provides better playmates for the children and better support for the parents. In fact, many MOPS and PEPS groups decide to turn into coops once the babies become toddlers

- Can anyone apply to join, or do prospects need to be referred by an existing member?

- Must the prospect attend a meeting prior to joining? (More on meetings later on.)

- Does the group vote on each prospect, or does the Moderator decide who is approved?

- If the group votes, does majority grant admittance or must there be unanimous agreement between members?

One important part of admitting members to any coop is the Home Visit. This should be a required part of the admittance process no matter how well your group knows the prospective member. The home visit should happen after a prospective member has expressed interest in the coop by attending a playgroup meeting.

During the home visit, two parents from the coop perform a safety check to validate that the home meets your requirements. Examples of things that you should check for include: screens on fireplaces, grounded electrical appliances, working smoke detectors, etc. A thorough home safety checklist can be found on the Kids Health website (www.kidshealth.org/parent) and is included in the back of this book.

Once the home visit is complete, the members who performed it should submit the results to the group Moderator along with a rating of "Pass" or "Fail." If the prospect fails the home visit, be sure to communicate those areas of concern to him/her. If the violations are minor, give the prospect the opportunity to fix the safety hazards within their home before rejecting the prospect outright. If the prospect passes the home visit – a hopefully more frequent scenario – spend a few minutes at the end of your visit reviewing the coop rules and operating procedures with the prospect. Make sure the prospect knows when and where the next meeting will be and understands that it is important to attend, as this will be his/her introduction to the group.

Create Roles

After you have determined how you will manage your coop (either with a coop site or using your own approach), you will determine what roles your coop needs, along with descriptions of responsibilities and length of tenure. The way that you have selected to manage your coop will dictate which roles you need to have. At a minimum, consider the following:

- **Moderator**: Oversees the coop operations. The Moderator is responsible for ensuring that regular meetings occur, managing the admittance of new members, and resolving disputes within the coop. Some coops refer to this position as Moderator.

- **Secretary** (*"do-it-yourself" only*): Arranges sits and tracks point balances. The Secretary is responsible for receiving sit requests from members, finding another member to fill those sit requests, and recording point exchanges between members.

For a site-managed coop, the only role you really need is the Moderator, as the site itself functions as Secretary. Each member should have a turn as the Moderator, with each turn lasting three – six months (three if your coop is small, six if it is large). Typically, members have their turn as Moderator according to the order in which they joined the coop. Once everyone has had a turn, circle back to the top of the list and start again. As new members join, they should be added to the bottom of the list.

By contrast, coops that have taken a "do-it-yourself" approach require both a Moderator and a Secretary. Depending on the sophistication of the coop's tools and processes, the amount of work that falls to the Secretary will vary. At a minimum, though, the Secretary must be responsible for the coop bookkeeping (i.e. making sure member balances accurately reflect all sits) and is often responsible for scheduling sits as well. Each member of the coop takes a turn as Secretary, but since this position entails a lot of work, members typically spend no more than three months at a time as Secretary. Additionally, many coops decide to "pay" the Secretary by giving that member a small amount of points for their service.

Sitting Compensation

The rules for how sittings are compensated vary slightly from coop to coop, but the fundamentals are the same. Members are credited points based on many different factors about the sitting they provided. Generally, members receive one point per child per hour of babysitting. In simple terms, that means if Joe watches Ellen's child for four hours, Joe receives four points (and Ellen is deducted four points, having "spent" them). Many coops elect to award half points for 30 minute increments and some even do quarter points for 15 minute increments. I would not recommend getting any more granular than 15 minutes. There are multiple situations, as well, where you may decide additional points are warranted. For example, you may consider awarding additional points to sitters who:

- Sit very late at night or very early in the morning
- Sit for multiple children
- Perform additional work, such as cleaning, serving dinner, giving baths, watching pets etc.
- Sit at the requesting member's home, as opposed to their own

It is very important that the rules for how points are calculated have been clearly outlined prior to the first sitting that occurs within your new coop. It doesn't really matter what the specific point rules are – what matters most is that all members understand them and are comfortable with them.

Point Corrections

Point corrections happen when the wrong number of points was transferred for a sit and you must fix it. There are two types of point corrections: undisputed corrections and disputed corrections. Undisputed corrections occur when both members (the requestor and the sitter) agree about the error and how to remedy it. In this case, members should handle the issue themselves by transferring the correct points to whoever is owed them.

If the requestor and the sitter are *not* in agreement over the number of points owed, you have what I call a disputed correction. If you're lucky, no members of your coop will ever have a disputed correction and you will never be called upon to settle a conflict. Unfortunately, life isn't perfect and disputes between members are inevitable. As the coop founder, it's important that you develop a process for handling disputed corrections (and communicate it to members) before the first one arises.

One method for dispute resolution is the "do nothing" approach, where the coop Moderator does not get involved except in very serious situations. Members are expected to resolve disputes themselves. If a member has an issue that does not get resolved, he/she may file a complaint with the Moderator against the offending party. After a certain number of complaints against a particular member, the Moderator may take decide to temporarily suspend that person's membership or to ban the member all together.

Another way to handle disputes is by granting the Moderator administrative power to adjust the points in such situations. This is the scenario I recommend. Here, the Moderator credits the slighted member with the balance in question. You may allow the Moderator to debit the offending member, as well, though this is naturally more contentious. The benefit of doing so is that it keeps the total number of points within the coop constant; the drawback of course is that you are deducting points from a member without their agreement, thus generating potential ill-sentiment. All corrections issued by the Moderator should be considered final.

Membership Fees

A great thing about babysitting coops is that they are essentially free. You will, however, want to require coop members to pay a small membership fee. Membership fees vary from coop to coop, with ranges generally between $10 and $25 per year. This fee will be used to cover expenses incurred over the course of the year. Typical expenses for a babysitting coop include: food and drinks for meetings, printing for handouts, etc. The participation fee for an online coop management site should be paid directly to the site by each member at the time s/he signs up. It should *not* be included in the membership fee paid to the coop.

Membership fees should be held together in a single bank account. This bank account should be in the coop's name, not the name of an individual, if possible. That will make it easier to transfer control of the account between members. The account should be managed be the current Moderator. The Moderator should maintain a historical record of all coop money that is spent. An easy way to do this is to get a debit card linked to the coop account – your bank will automatically keep a record of all debit transactions and you don't have to worry about spreadsheets or checkbook balancing. If your coop is pretty small, a dedicated bank account may be overkill. If you opt not to go the bank account route, just be diligent to keep extremely good records of the money coming and going.

As referenced above, online coop management sites usually charge a site usage fee in exchange for handling the day-to-day operations of your coop (as well as for providing many other benefits which are detailed later on). This site usage fee is in addition to the coop membership fee; however, since these sites remove a large part of the offline work (no secretary scheduling sits, no tracking points via spreadsheet, etc.), they also lower the coop membership cost. The total membership cost (coop membership fee plus site usage fee, if applicable) is usually about the same, whether or not your group takes advantage of a coop management site.

To determine what your coop's membership fee ought to be, you should create an estimated budget. Determine what expenses your coop will have. Expenses include everything from food for meetings to printing costs. Then estimate how many members your coop will have. Divide the number of members by the total anticipated expenses for the year, and then add an additional ten percent to that. This will be the amount you should charge each member. The reason that I recommend adding ten percent is that unplanned expenses always arise, and it is far better to have a little extra on hand to cover them than to have to ask members for more money later on.

Recruiting Members

Now that you've created your new coop, it's time to start recruiting and admitting members. After all, the coop won't be of much value unless people join and participate in it. Thankfully, there are many tools available to you that will help you find the right members and broadcast your new coop to them.

Plan an Initial Meeting

The first thing you'll want to do is plan an initial meeting for prospective members to meet one another and to get information from you on what the coop is all about. Select a location for the meeting and a time that you envision to be convenient for most people – for example, if your prospective members consist primarily of working moms, you'll want to schedule the meeting in the evening or on a weekend.

The purpose of this initial meeting is two-fold. First, you'll want the prospective members to have an opportunity to meet and socialize with one another. For your coop to be successful, it is extremely important that members are comfortable with everyone else in the group. After all, they will be entrusting these people to care for their children. Make sure you leave time at the end of the meeting for casual conversation.

Second, you'll want to provide an overview to the group on the purpose of your babysitting coop and how you envision it working. Among the prospective members there will likely be a wide range of understanding on the topic of babysitting coops. Some will have barely heard the term before, while others might have participated in coops in the past (and thus have their own views about the way a coop should be run). Your goal should be to get all prospects on the same page, presenting to them how this coop will be run. Don't be a dictator, though. Even though you created the coop, your prospective members will probably have their own thoughts and ideas on how they think the coop should operate. Listen to what they have to say, and engage in an open dialogue with the group.

For the initial meeting, I recommend you limit it to adults. A lot of coops have regular meetings where kids are invited – and actually encouraged – to attend. For future meetings, I'd recommend doing the same. However, since this first one is about parents getting to know one another, having the chance to talk and ask questions, and ultimately evaluating whether they'd like to join the coop, you'll want to ask them to keep the kids at home.

Target Prospective Members

The best way to target prospective members will depend on who the people you want to target are. Do you have a target demographic in mind, or specific individuals? How well do you know them? Are you connected to any of these people via social networking sites? Do you have their email addresses? Are you looking for a core group of people to recommend their friends, or do you already have a plethora of people to join?

First, you'll need to inform prospects about your upcoming introductory meeting. This is a chance for prospects to learn more about your coop, including what benefits they would get, how it will work, and why they should join. The less you know these people on an individual level, the more you'll want to stress the value of the coop in your communication to them.

- **Email / Evite**: For prospects you know well and whose email addresses you have, you should contact them directly. The best way to do this is through a personal email that gives a quick overview of what the coop is and invites them to the first meeting. Don't feel like you need to write a new email to each individual – craft the email once and then just swap out the name at the top before you send it. An alternative to email is sending an evite (an amalgamation of "electronic" and "invite"). Evites allow prospects to see who has else been invited and who is planning to attend. People feel more comfortable attending an event when they have an idea of whom else will be there – it lets them mentally prepare and it increases their likelihood of attending. Currently, there are many sites where you can create and send evites: Evite (www.evite.com), Anyvite (www.anyvite.com), MyPunchbowl (www.mypunchbowl.com), Pingg (www.pingg.com) – to name a few.

- **Social Networking Sites:** There are many tools out there today that allow you to connect with friends, family, and others with similar interests. In fact, it's highly likely that you are already using one or more social networking tools in your everyday life. Why not leverage these rich connections to grow your coop? Two sites I especially like for this purpose are Facebook and Meetup.

    o *Facebook*: For prospects that you know moderately to very well, Facebook (www.facebook.com) is an extremely useful tool. The social networking site allows you to create groups – which may be either public or private, depending on your preference – and invite others to join them. You can also create events and invitations, which is a terrific way to publicize your meeting to not only your prospective members but to all their friends as well. When prospects confirm that they will attend, it shows up in the "newsfeed" of their contacts – many of whom may likely be in the same target demographic as your prospects and interested in joining as well.

- *Meetup*: Another networking site worth utilizing is Meetup (www.meetup.com). Unlike Facebook, Meetup is more beneficial with prospects you may only know as acquaintances or not at all. Meetup is a site that allows people to locate groups in their area based on specific interests. By listing your group on Meetup, you can publicize your new coop and your upcoming meeting to people in your area who are already interested in joining a coop (and who might not otherwise have known about your group). The only drawback to Meetup is that there is a monthly subscription fee for listing a group on their site, so you'll want to be fairly confident that you are going to utilize it when you sign up.

- **Community Blogs / Parenting Sites:** A great way to find prospective members is to write something for your local community blog, showcasing your new coops and the benefits of being a member. The people who read community blogs tend to be, not surprisingly, very community-oriented individuals – a perfect target audience! Plus, community blogs have been growing rapidly in popularity recently.

More and more people are looking to them as the authoritative source on what's happening in their area.

Don't have a community blog in your area? Check out some of the many parenting sites that exist and reach out to local "Mommy / Daddy Bloggers." Chances are, the people who run these sites would love to have you help you promote your group and provide valuable information to their readership at the same time.

- **Print Flyers:** I know, I know. It sounds archaic, right? But depending on your prospects, printed flyers may prove surprisingly effective. If you have a target community in mind – a school, a neighborhood, etc. – but don't know have specific individuals in mind, using strategically placed flyers will advertise your coop in an informative yet unobtrusive manner.

Keep your message concise (if it's too long, people might not stop long enough to read it) and clearly elucidate the value. Make sure to include your contact info and encourage people to reach out to you with questions. An easy way to include contact info is by printing it at the bottom of your flier on multiple, perforated tear-aways – think of those fliers you see by the entrance to the supermarket.

That allows people to grab your name and number if they're interested, rather than trying to find a paper and pen on the spot. As far as placement goes, choose a spot where people will see them and, ideally, where people are forced to slow down anyway. For example, at my son's daycare, parents are required to stop by the office to sign their kids in and out. Because parents have to stop there twice a day as part of their normal routine, the bulletin board directly above the sign-in folders is a prime spot for posting fliers and relevant information.

- **Referrals**: Finally, utilize the good prospects you *do* know to identify the prospects you don't know. To the extent possible, I encourage you to grow your coop organically through referrals. Encourage the founding members and prospects you've already identified to invite a few friends each. They say you can tell a lot about a person by the friends they keep. Since the prospects you invited are people you think highly of, it is likely that their friends would be of similar character and would be people you'd want in your coop as well. Referrals are one the best ways of growing your coop. Encouraging new members to refer others strengthens and reinforces their bond to the group by leveraging their already existing personal relationships. Also, it is an extremely efficient way of finding good prospects in whom there is already at least a moderate level of trust (since one or more members know this person pretty well).

Conduct the Initial Meeting

You've planned for it, you've targeted prospects, and you've communicated information about your initial coop get together. Now it's time to actually have the meeting! The meeting should be about two hours long. Two hours will allow enough time for: people to arrive and settle (15 minutes), an overview of the coop and how you envision it running (30 minutes), questions and answers from the prospective members (45 minutes), and mingling at the end (30 minutes).

Try as best you can to make sure you know who is planning to attend. Ideally, have name tags ready for people to take as they arrive. Whether or not you have a list of attendees, make sure you have plenty of blank name tags on hand – people will likely bring friends you did not know about (which is a good thing!). Also make sure you provide some light snacks and beverages. This should be a relatively informal and fun meeting, and you want people to walk away from the meeting with a positive impression and the feeling that this is a group they'd like to be a part of.

At the end of the meeting, make sure there is a sheet available where people may express their level of interest in joining your coop. Those who definitely want to join the coop must sign this sheet before leaving the meeting. That way, after the initial meeting, you will have a list of people who are interested in joining and whom you can consider for membership.

Hopefully, almost all of the people who attend your meeting will be people you'd consider for membership, but this is not always the case. Meet with your co-founders (i.e. the friends you formed the coop with) and review the prospective members. You should admit as many members as you desire. A coop benefits from having more members (to a point, of course), as it increases the number of sitters and the likelihood that someone will be available when a member needs it. One thing note: unless a prospect is a personal friend or someone you know very well, you should not admit them until *after* performing a home visit. (More on home visits below.)

Once you've made the decision of whom to admit, communicate both the admissions and denials right away. If you do deny prospects, make sure you are diplomatic about it, so that you leave them with a positive feeling toward your group and don't create an awkward social situation for yourself later on. For those you admit, welcome them warmly and invite them to attend a formal meeting of the new coop – the first Business Meeting. This will be a chance for the new members of the coop to come together and meet more intimately those parents with whom they will be swapping sits. It will also be the time that you agree upon coop rules as a group. More about Business Meetings and establishing rules is below.

Establish Rules

At the outset, you will need to establish coop rules. This should be done at your first coop Business Meeting, once new members have been admitted. It's better to go through the process of setting rules as a group than to do it completely by yourself. Setting rules as a group gets buy-in from members and makes them less likely to disagree with a policy down the road.

Of course, it would be highly inefficient and a good use of no one's time for members to brainstorm coop rules from scratch. Instead, you should create a well-documented list of suggested rules. Before the meeting, distribute a copy of the suggested rules to each member and ask them to review it. During the meeting you will run down the list, discussing each rule as a group and encouraging members to provide feedback and / or suggested changes. Establishing the rules this way allows you to be respectful of members' time, while also enabling them to participate in the rule generation process. At the back of this book, I have included a list of my recommended coop rules. Feel free to use this as your starting point and amend it to fit the needs of your coop.

Hold Monthly Playgroups

One day every month (or every few months) – preferably a weekend, so that working parents can attend without being unduly inconvenienced – coops should have a playgroup meeting. The playgroup meeting should occur on the same day and time each month so that parents can plan in advance to attend them. Select a playgroup spot that works for your coop. The local park or playground is a popular choice for many coops. And for days when the weather just doesn't cooperate, many cities also have indoor gyms where kids can play for a small fee. Another option is to have your playgroup at a member's home – but be warned: this option really only works if your coop is ten members or less.

Playgroups are an opportunity for new prospects to check out your coop and determine if they have an interest in joining the group. Because of this, try to hold playgroups in the same location each time and clearly communicate where they will be. You want to make it as stress-free as possible for prospects to find and visit with your group. While the kids play, the prospect will have the opportunity to talk with other parents and find out what your coop is all about. During the playgroup - or at any time after – the prospect may communicate that he or she is interested in joining. At that point, the Moderator will schedule a home visit for the prospect.

Current coop members should be encouraged, but

not required, to attend playgroups. For obvious reasons, playgroups tend to be more popular in coops where there are a lot of younger children. If your coop tends to have older children or to have a wide variety of ages, you may wish to consider an alternate venue for meeting prospective members.

Plan Business Meetings

Your coop should plan to hold regular business meetings once every three months. You may decide your group needs to hold them more or less often, but in my experience, every three months seems to be the right frequency for most coops. Be consistent about when these meetings will occur, so that members can plan accordingly. Usually, the first Tuesday evening of the month is a good time – it avoids most major holidays and holding the meeting in the evening allows working parents to attend. Meetings can be as formal or informal as you like. These meetings will be for conducting any and all coop business. Such business may include, but not be limited to: reviewing rules and procedures, assigning new roles, and voting on prospective members.

The coop Moderator is responsible for setting the agenda and making sure all topics on the agenda are covered. These meetings will give members a chance to get together as a group, free of other distraction. Most coops conduct business meetings without kids, so that members can devote their full attention to any matters at hand. This is not the time for socialization. The regular playgroups should provide sufficient opportunity for coop children to become familiar with the adults who will be caring for them and the other children they will be spending time with.

Since business meetings do not occur frequently, it is important that as many individuals as possible attend. One way to encourage attendance is to deduct a small amount of points from each member who does not attend a coop business meeting. (My coop requires you attend every third. You are docked points after you have missed three meetings in a row.) If you decide to do this, be sure to apply this deduction consistently. Do not attempt to determine "how good" someone's excuse is for missing a meeting. It will lead to feelings of favoritism. Either everyone who misses a meeting loses points, or no one does. The single exception to this is for those parents unable to find childcare – if a parent cannot attend a meeting due to lack of childcare, that member should not be docked points.

Admitting Members on an Ongoing Basis

As I mentioned above, you should require that any and all prospective members to your coop attend one of your monthly playgroups as a prerequisite to joining. Under no circumstances should you admit a new member to the coop without giving the existing members a chance to meet him or her. Remember, this is a person that your coop members must feel comfortable entrusting their children's safety to – it is absolutely essential that the members have met and are comfortable with a new prospect.

You should feel free to develop a new member admittance process that works best for your particular coop. Here is one process that I have seen be very successful, as it provides necessary checks and balances without being overly complicated.

1. **Prospect attends a monthly playgroup meeting.** The prospect should bring his or her children to a monthly playgroup meeting. Here, the prospect will have the chance to talk with coop members, learn more about the group, and determine if there is mutual interest.

2. **Coop conducts a home visit.** Two coop members arrange a home visit with the prospective member. During this visit, the coop members conduct a thorough safety check of the prospect's home. They also review the coop rules and procedures with the prospect at this time.

3. **Members vote at next business meeting.** At the next business meeting, present the prospect as a

candidate for membership. According to the rules you have created for voting, determine whether to admit the prospect into your coop. Once a decision has been made, the Moderator should communicate it to the prospect. Note: If your next business meeting is months away, consider have an ad-hoc voting session to decide on the prospect.

4. **Distribute forms, collect fees, and enroll member.** At this point, your prospect becomes a member and needs to complete all the necessary forms for enrollment – such as the medical authorization form, emergency contact form, etc. Collect the completed forms along with the coop membership fee. If your coop is using an online coop site, instruct the member on how to create an account there. Add the new member to all mailing list and group contact information.

5. **Invite member to attend next business meeting.** Once a member has been enrolled, he/she is invited to attend the next business meeting so that everyone has a chance to welcome this new individual as a full-fledged member. Be sure to introduce the new member warmly and allow time at the end of the meeting for socialization.

Once step four is completed, the prospect becomes a full member of your coop and is expected to attend all regular meetings. Depending on the roles you have created for your coop, he or she may eventually have a turn at being the Moderator and/or Secretary. However, be careful not to assign too much responsibility to new members early on. At the beginning, their focus should be on getting to know the other members in the group and becoming comfortable swapping sits. It takes a little while for many people to feel comfortable enough with someone else that they entrust them with the care of their children. Let new members ease into the coop at their own pace.

Safety Tip: Be extra diligent when assessing prospects you found through advertising as opposed to through someone in your network. Ask these prospects for multiple referrals, so that you can talk to people they know. Spend more time during the home visit getting a sense for who they are. Above all, trust your instincts. If something seems off or you aren't completely comfortable with a prospect, say no. Much better to let a prospect down than to risk your children's safety.

Be conscious of the size of your coop at any given point in time. As families leave the coop, make sure you are actively recruiting new families to take their place. A coop without enough participants will not smoothly. The number of families you need in your coop depends on how actively members use it. The more active your members are, the fewer members you need to have.

If you notice that your coop size is starting to dwindle, enlist the help of your members to recruit new families. Tell them to think about their neighbors, their friends, the people their children attend school with. It's a good idea to have a sample email that they can use to contact new recruits – in this email, be sure to include some basic information about your coop, a link to your coop's public information page (on your coop management site), and the contact information for the current Moderator. Having a sample email ready to go will make it easy for members to reach out, as well as ensure the consistency of information disseminated.

Your Coop in Action

Using a Coop Site

One of the reasons you started this coop was to make your life easier, right? Well, what's easy about having to call a coop secretary every time you need a sitter? What's easy about having to be the secretary when your turn comes due, making rounds of calls (or sending rounds of emails) every single time a member needs a sitter? What's easy about not being able to see your point balance or monitor your transaction history for accuracy? Quite frankly, an offline coop creates almost as much work as it saves.

By utilizing a coop management website like we recommend, you will reduce the number of manual tasks you perform and nearly eliminate human error. This chapter walks you through the ongoing operations of an online coop (for operating a coop without a coop site, please see the next chapter). Follow the advice here, and your coop should be running like a well-oiled machine in no time.

Joining a Site

Once you've joined the site and set up your coop, you'll

need to invite your coop members to join it as well. You can use the site to send email invitations to your members, and these invitations will include a direct link to joining the online coop. Once at the site, they will be prompted to become members of the site before they can join your coop. Becoming a member of the site very is easy – all they need to do is fill out some basic contact information. Most sites charge a membership fee; this fee is comparable to or less than what most coops charge for annual memberships. Because most of the coop administration is handled by the site (and not a coop secretary), you can reduce the amount you charge in annual memberships. As a result, online coops tend to cost about the same as their offline counterparts, but they remove a lot of the work involved.

One important part of the membership creation process is specifying email preferences. Members will have the option of determining what information gets emailed to them and how frequently. For instance, a member may want to receive an email every time someone responds to a sitting request she created, but may only want to receive a list of the new requests created by other members once per day (in digest form). Although members should think carefully about their email preferences on sign up, these email preferences can be easily changed at any time.

After members have joined the site, they will request to become a part of the coop you created. This can be done one of two ways: either by clicking a link that has been emailed to them (mentioned above) or by searching for the coop on the site and clicking a "join now" button. By using an invitation link, you are pre-approving a member to be part of the coop and, upon clicking that link, the member is instantly granted access. If the member reaches your coop through a search instead of an emailed link, that works, too. However, instead of getting instant access to the coop, the member has to wait until the Moderator (likely, you) approves them.

Creating a Sit Request

Creating a sit request ("request") is quite intuitive when using an online site like SittingAround. After clicking on the link to create a new request, members fill out the details of the sitting needed. These details include: number and ages of children, date, time, location (sitter's home, requester's home, or other), special instructions, etc. Once a member has created the request, it will be posted on the coop's home page under "Open Requests" and will be emailed to coop members according to their email preferences.

Requests can be edited as needed prior to being assigned to a sitter. Changes to the request will not be emailed to coop members, but will display when a member views the request on the website. When logged in to the site, the requesting member will be able to view all the sitting requests he/she has created, as well as the status of those requests (sitter assigned, not fulfilled, etc.).

Fulfilling a Sit Request

After viewing a sit request on the site, a member will have the option of messaging the requester with additional questions or offering to fulfill the sit request. Multiple members may offer to fulfill a single request. The requesting member will be able to view all offers and accept whichever one he/she chooses.

Generally, a member will accept the first request that is received; however, there may be scenarios where preference is given to specific offers. That is okay! In old-school coops, the member who had the least amount of points would be given the chance to fulfill the request first, followed by the members with the next fewest points and so on down the list. While this kept the points balance relatively equal between members, it did not allow the requester much say in who cared for their kids.

There are very good reasons for wanting to choose a sitter – such as the ability to select someone who has kids of a similar age or someone who lives in close proximity to the requesting member. The whole point of a babysitting coop is to make life easier for its members, not harder. The ability to select which offer to accept does that. That said, if this system becomes problematic – members playing favorites, certain individuals rarely having the ability to sit, etc. – you will need to revise the process and make it more prescribed.

Depending on their email preferences, requesters may be notified whenever someone offers to fulfill their sit request. Receiving real-time notifications allows requesters to respond quickly and confirm a sitter. It also allows them to change the status of their request, indicating to the rest of the group that a sitter has been found (and thus they will not waste their time offering). Once a sitter has been selected, the status of the sit request changes from "open" to "fulfilled."

Transferring Points

Once the date for a scheduled sitting has passed, the requesting member will receive an email prompt to transfer the appropriate number of points to the member that provided the sitting services. By clicking on the prompt in the email, the requesting member will be taken to the point transfer form. This form will be pre-populated with the amount of points to be transferred, as calculated from the request. If the amount of points is accurate, all the requesting member needs to do is click to transfer and the sitting is complete.

  Fairly often, the amount of sitting provided will be slightly more or slightly less than the estimate provided in the request. Maybe the requesting member ran late or maybe they only wound up needing sitting for one child instead of two. Because of this common occurrence, the point transfer form will be editable. The requesting member can adjust the number of points, up or down, before completing the transfer.

If the requesting member does not complete the transfer

within a certain period of time after the sitting occurred, the number of points calculated from the original request will be *automatically* transferred to the sitter. At that point, it will be the responsibility of the requesting member to transfer any potential additional points manually; likewise, if a sitter is overpaid, it will be the sitter's responsibility to transfer any overpaid points back to the requesting member. In the case of a member forgetting or possibly refusing to transfer points, the member who is owed the points may appeal to the Moderator. The Moderator will have administrative power to intervene and resolve the dispute.

Do-It-Yourself Coop Management

A do-it-yourself approach to coop management provides an alternative to the site-based model, especially for groups whose members are not as comfortable using the internet or do not have regular access to a computer. Though more and more coops are utilizing specific coop websites these days, there are still a sizable number of coops that operate successfully without one. Operating such a coop requires a time investment from the Moderator and the coop secretary, along with a set of more prescriptive processes for its members. In this chapter, I outline some of the best practices for managing a do-it-yourself coop to its fullest (and least labor-intensive) potential.

For clarification, I will be using the term "do-it-yourself" coop to denote any coop that is run without the aid of a specific coop website.

Creating a Piecemeal Online Solution

Using a variety of online tools, you can cobble together a system that performs each of the necessary tasks of running a coop. The reason many people do this is because they think they can create a good enough system for managing their coop via free online tools.

While this approach may save a few dollars for your members, it is not without drawbacks and in many areas, these drawbacks are significant. Unlike a coop specific website, amalgamated solutions have sit requests and point tracking tools that are not integrated. This means that every time a sit is completed in one tool, someone has to go over to the point tracking tool and create a record of it. (It won't happen automatically.) This approach can be cumbersome for novices, and advanced users often wind up frustrated at the lack of integration between the tools. There are security concerns, and each time you add a member, you need to make sure they are added to each of the component tools within your system. For those who want to truly build it themselves, here are some tools you can use to do it.

- **Yahoo / Google / Facebook Groups** allow members to communicate with one another through a single medium. Communication is typically public, viewable by all members of the group. Depending on your settings, information may be viewable by others outside the group.

- **Reply-All Mailing Lists** allow members to communicate with one another through an email list. Communication is viewable to all members of the group, but not to anyone else. You will need to be diligent about adding new members to the mailing list – forgetting to do so would mean they would miss important coop communication.

- **Online Document Sharing Tools** provide coops with the ability to share documents such as sitting schedules and point totals with the group. Most document-sharing tools allow you to set user-based permissions – you can limit who is able to view vs. modify the files. However, for the documents to be current, someone must remember to update them. These tools are good for tracking points but not good for scheduling sits. Additionally, privacy can be an issue and a novice user could accidentally delete important information.

- **Meetup / Event Scheduling Sites** allow you to create events for specific groups and broadcast them. You can advertise upcoming events or get-togethers, such as playgroups, to people in the community. Meetup is a good way to advertise the existence of your coop to prospects and to notify members of upcoming events at the same time. Just be careful that you do not share any private or sensitive information on a publically viewable site.

Creating a Sit Request

When a member wants to create a sit request, he/she contacts the current Secretary. The requesting member communicates all important information to the Secretary, such as: number and ages of children, date, time, location (sitter's home, requester's home, or other), special instructions, etc. The Secretary records this information in the form of a sit request. Based on the information provided, the Secretary informs the requesting member how many points the sit will "cost." It is then the Secretary's responsibility to find a member to fulfill the sit request.

Some coops allow members to coordinate sits directly with one another. This works okay, so long as members are diligent about communicating any such sits to the Secretary. In this scenario, a member typically sends an email request out to the entire coop (i.e. "Looking for a sitter to Thursday, October 12th"). While the Secretary does not have to be the one coordinating sits, but he/she does need to maintain a record of all transactions, at a minimum.

Fulfilling a Sit Request

The Secretary has a list of all coop members and their respective point balances. When a sit request comes in, the Secretary starts by contacting the member with the fewest points first and offering that member the opportunity to fulfill the request. Doing so gives the members with the fewest points the opportunity to earn more, thus keeping a more even point distribution among members of the coop.

If the member with the fewest points is able to sit, the Secretary informs the requesting member that a sitter has been found and provides the sitters name and contact info to the requesting member. At this point, the requesting member and the sitter coordinate further details of the sit between themselves. If the member with the fewest points is not available to sit, the Secretary contacts the member with the next fewest points (and so on down the list), until a sitter is found.

Alternatively, if the member has sent an email request out to the entire coop, members may respond directly to the requestor (who will confirm the selected sitter). This gives the requestor greater say over who sits for them and is a faster way to communicate a new sit to the group; the single drawback, though, is that members responding to a sit have no way of knowing whether it has already been filled.

Transferring Points

Option One: It is the Secretary's job to keep track of all sittings that take place within the coop and to make sure that the corresponding points are transferred among members. It is the requesting member's job, however, to confirm that a sit took place. The reason the requesting member must do this (as opposed to the sitter) is because the points come out of the requesting member's account. Think of it like paying an actual babysitter – you, as the parent, must voluntarily pay your sitter for their services once they have been rendered. Though the sitter is rightfully due the payment, he / she cannot go into your wallet and simply take the money. The same principles apply in a coop – the requesting member must contact the Secretary to "pay" (i.e. give points) to the member who sat for them.

Once the sit has been completed, the requesting member is required to contact the Secretary to: 1) confirm that the sit took place, and 2) communicate the correct points to transfer to the sitter (sits often go longer or shorter than initially estimated). That gives the Secretary permission to transfer the points and to mark the sit as recorded. (Recorded means that the points have been transferred). If the requesting member forgets to contact the Secretary within 24 hours after the sit took place, the Secretary will mark the sit as recorded and transfer the amount of points based on the original request. If the amount of points is incorrect, as it often will be, it is up to either the requesting member or the sitter to inform the

Secretary. Note: Additional points can only be given to the sitter upon agreement from the requesting member or through the intervention of the Moderator (in the case of a dispute).

Without a specific coop site, the process of transferring points is quite manual, but there are ways to ease the burden. The simplest way to do this is for the Secretary to maintain transactions and point transfers via a spreadsheet. If possible, store the spreadsheet on a free document collaboration site. You can share the spreadsheet and any other documents with your coop – if you wanted, you could set permissions so that the entire coop could view the spreadsheet and make sure all their sits have been accurately recorded.

Option Two: Some coops negate the need for a Secretary by distributing a specific amount of poker chips or some other non-monetary currency to each member upon joining the coop. When a sit has been completed, the requesting member literally pays the sitter – only instead of using actual money, the requesting member pays in coop currency.

While this system eases the burden on the Secretary, it increases the burden on individual members, who are now responsible for keeping track of their coop currency. For organized people, this likely won't be a great concern. However, in the event that coop currency is lost or that someone cannot remember whether they were paid for a sit, there exists no record of the transaction (and thus, no recourse). Also, if you use this system, be careful, for obvious reasons, not to use monopoly money as your currency or any other easily replicable currency.

Forms and Documentation

As you create and operate your coop, you will want to make sure that you collect all necessary information from each member. In addition to making your life easier, doing so will protect you and your members from preventable liability. Below, I detail what each form or piece of documentation is and why you need it. At the end of this book, you will find samples of some coop forms. Please feel free to photocopy them as needed and use them within your coop.

Membership Form

This form need not be complicated, nor need it communicate each and every rule your coop has. The purpose of this form is to outline the general principles that members agree to abide by. It's more of a formality than anything else, but having new members complete the membership form marks their official entrance into your coop. At the time they sign up, they should also receive a copy of the coop's by-laws, which provides the rules in detail.

Homeowners Insurance

It is important that each member of your coop have homeowners' (or renters') liability insurance. This will protect members in the event that a child or another member is injured in their home during a sit. Homeowners' liability insurance contains two forms of coverage: personal liability insurance and medical payments to others. Personal liability insurance covers you against lawsuits that may arise due to someone being harmed on your property. This harm could refer to personal injury or to property damage. This coverage usually pays for your appearance in court, should that be necessary. The second type of coverage, medical payments to others, does exactly what it sounds like. This coverage pays for treatments to those who have become injured on your property. Treatments can include doctors' visits, x-rays, hospital stays, etc.

Medical Treatment Authorization

In the event that your child becomes ill while in the care of a coop member, you will want to be sure you have completed a medical treatment authorization form. Completing this form allows the coop member to provide emergency medical care to your child, should he/she need it. It is standard practice for any organization providing childcare to require such authorization; virtually every daycare or sports team I have come across has made the medical treatment authorization mandatory.

At a minimum, this form should contain your child's basic health information (any known allergies, medications, etc.), emergency contact information, doctor and dentist contact information, and your signature. Make certain that this form expressly indicates that you authorize the caregiver to provide emergency medical assistance in your absence. Don't worry about completing a new form for each member who joins the coop – instead, be sure to specify on your form that by authorizing the coop itself, you thereby authorize any and all of its members.

It is extremely important that all coop members complete a medical treatment form before they schedule sits. Should a child become ill, you want the sitter able to respond to the situation, focused only on caring for the child. You do not want the sitter worrying about potential liabilities of treating a child for whom a medical treatment form has not yet been signed.

Gun Safety Policy

Improperly stored guns pose a serious risk to children in the home. Some coops elect to inform all members about the presence of guns in a home; others refuse to grant membership to families with guns in the home altogether. If you do permit members who own guns, be sure that this fact is understood by all members of your coop. All coop members should be required to declare any guns in their homes and must agree to a set of gun safety rules set forth by the coop.

Commonly Asked Questions

How much can I expect to save with a babysitting coop?

That depends upon a number of factors – namely, what average babysitting rates are in your area and how often you use a sitter. For a family paying $10 per hour and using a sitter twice a month (assuming 5 hours each time), they could expect to save $1,200 each year!

How do I find a coop in my area?

Go to SittingAround (www.sittingaround.com) and enter your zip code. Your search results will display a list of coops near you, as well as a link to their public information page. If you see a coop that you may be interested in joining, send a message to the Moderator.

What if I can't find a coop near me?

Start your own! Starting your own coop does require a bit of work upfront, but you'll be pleasantly surprised at how quickly and how well your efforts pay off.

How do I make my child comfortable having many different sitters?

I focus less on the sitter and more on the sitter's child(ren). Instead of positioning it as "You're having a babysitter," position it as "You're going to Olivia's house to play. "In fact, at our house, we never even call it the Babysitting Coop – we've renamed it "The Friends Come Over and Play Club." My son loves playing with other children, so participating in "The Club" is a special treat for him.

I have noticed, as well, that many children are more at ease when they know their sitter is someone else's Mommy or Daddy. There is something comforting – especially to younger children – about being in the care of another family.

I've had a dispute over a sit. The Moderator sided with the other member and I think it's because they are good friends. What do I do?

It is the Moderator's job to be a completely unbiased party and to make decisions based strictly on the facts. We're all human, though, and sometimes our biases affect us without us realizing it. If you suspect that is the case, talk to the Moderator and explain your concern. Most likely, she'll be apologetic. If she continues to display preferential behavior, however, you should bring it up with other coop members. In the most serious of cases, a Moderator who cannot exhibit fair judgment should be removed from her position.

Is it okay to only swap sits with certain members of the coop?

That's a delicate issue and it depends a lot on your particular circumstances. It's a lot easier to be selective about who you swap sits with when you're in a larger coop. In a small coop, it's more noticeable and the potential for hurt feelings increases. That said, one of the great things about a coop is that you have many sitters to choose from. You shouldn't feel bad about giving preference to a member who has kids close in age to yours, nor should you feel obligated to accept the first sit offer you receive.

What if I need to cancel a sit last minute?

If you cancel a sit more than 24 hours ahead of time, there should be no repercussions. However, if you cancel a sit within the 24-hour window, you should be required to pay the other party (sitter or requestor) half the number of points that the sit was worth. So, if you cancel a sit that would have cost 30 points, you would have to pay 15 points to the other member. You may choose to waive this penalty on a case-by-case basis. Similarly, you may have allowable cancellation reasons – such as a family emergency – where the cancelling party does not get penalized. If you do have allowable reasons, make sure you put a cap on how many times a member may claim them without penalty.

Should members be allowed to go negative in their point balance?

Yes. Think about it – a member has 0 points, is planning to build his points back up, and then an emergency situation arises and he needs a sitter. You should put a cap on how many points negative a member may go. My coop allows members to go 100 points negative. At that point, the member must sit for others and reduce his debt before he may schedule another sitter for himself. Putting a cap on how negative a member may go also mitigates the harm that could be caused by someone who joins the coop, goes hugely negative, and then disappears without repaying their debt.

What do I do if a member wants to leave the coop?

Members come and go over time. Perhaps the children got

old enough to no longer need a sitter. Or, maybe the members weren't getting what they needed out of the coop. Whatever the reason, a member should be able to leave your coop at any time. If a member has a positive point balance at the time of their departure, those points automatically go into the coop float account. If a member has a negative balance at the time of their departure, they should be required to either work off their debt (the encouraged option) or reimburse the coop for their debt. The reimbursement rate is up to you, but I think $1 per point is reasonable.

Conclusion

I hope that this book has introduced you to the wonderful world of babysitting coops and given you the tools you need to find or start your own. Parenting is a demanding job. The more support you have around you, the easier that job becomes – and the better you are at it. When you have a group of families nearby who are ready to sit for you when you need it (or just when you want it), breaks are easier to take. Scheduling a sitter is no longer a stressful experience, nor is it an expensive one. A play date for your child becomes a time for you to go to an appointment, see a movie, take a nap – or virtually anything else you want to do.

Since joining and participating in a babysitting coop, I have never been more pleased with the quality of care I get from my sitters. Similarly, when I sit for others, I feel happy that I am able to provide a safe and trusted environment for my neighbors' children. The money that I save by being in the coop (which I estimate to have been $1,500 for my family last year alone) is just the icing on the cake.

My son loves being part of the coop, too. It has allowed him to get to know other kids in the neighborhood – something that will serve him well as he prepares to start at our local elementary school. And, it has provided a network of trusting families for me, families that I can lean on for parenting advice, friendship, and support. Now that we have been a part of this network, I cannot imagine my life without it. The idea of hiring a paid sitter – once my only form of childcare – is the furthest thought from my mind. Why would I pay for a sitter when I can get better ones for free?

      Which, of course begs the question, why would you?

For more information on starting a babysitting coop, including tools and advice, please visit SittingAround (www.sittingaround.com).

Appendix

Sample New Member Contract

I, (We) agree to:

1. Read and abide by the bylaws and safety recommendations.
2. Be responsible for arranging my own sits.
3. Maintain my own records of points to validate against the coop site at the end of each month.
4. Attend monthly coop meetings. Be responsible for finding out what business occurred at any missed meetings. I understand that under the bylaws I will be docked 10 points for each meeting thereafter until a meeting I attended.
5. Contribute towards group expenses such as food and site membership.
6. Provide the sitter with an emergency medical form for my child/children.
7. Assume the duties of Moderator when it is my turn.
8. Try to pass through zero points every three months. If I reach negative 50 points, I agree to actively seek opportunities to work off points. If I reach positive 50 points, I agree to spend the points in a timely fashion.

9. Pledge to leave the coop with a zero or positive balance or pay off negative points at $1.00 per point, or in some other manner to be decided by the membership. Funds will go to the group treasury.

10. Disclose the presence of a gun(s) in my(our) house.
    - I(We) DO   DO NOT (circle one) Have a gun(s) in my house
    - If yes, I(We) agree to keep it (them) unloaded and in a locked place, with ammunition stored separately.

Parent 1 Name (print)

_____

Parent 2 Name (print)

_____

Address

_____

Telephone

_____

E-mail address

_____

Children name(s) and birthday(s)

_____

Sign _____

Date _____

Sample Coop By-Laws

1. DEFINITIONS

    1.1. Requester: The member leaving children in a sitter's care

    1.2. Sitter: The member caring for the requester's children

    1.3. Moderator: The temporary leader of the coop, responsible for planning meetings and resolving disputes. Each member will have a turn in this role, with each turn lasting a period of three months.

    1.4. Points: The coop currency that is exchanged for sits. One hour of babysitting for one child = one point.

2. MEMBERSHIP REQUIREMENTS

    2.1. Coop Boundaries. Prospective members must reside between (east) Street and (west) Street, and between (north) Street and (south) Street. Prospective members on the border may be considered on a case-by-case basis.

2.2. Prospective members must attend one playgroup meeting to be considered for admission.

2.3. Prospective members must pass a home visit inspection to be considered for admission.

2.4. If a prospective member meets the above criteria, the current membership will vote on the prospective member at the next business meeting. Majority vote grants admission.

2.5. To join the coop, the prospective member must complete all required forms and pay the membership fee. He/she must agree to abide by all coop rules.

3. MEDICAL CARE AND HOME SAFETY

   3.1. Members are required to have and show proof of comprehensive homeowners' or renters' liability insurance.

   3.2. Members must complete a Medical Treatment Authorization form for each child who may receive care from a coop sitter.

   3.3. Members are required to have an immunization record for each child who may receive care from a coop sitter.

3.4. Members must disclose whether they own a gun. Members who own guns must sign and comply with a gun safety form.

3.5. No member will utilize the coop or provide services when there is a contagious illness in their home. Sitters may refuse to sit, penalty-free, due to a contagious illness in the requester's home.

3.6. The coop may suspend or terminate a member at any time if that member's home is deemed unsafe.

4. MEETINGS AND PLAYGROUPS

    4.1. Business Meetings

       4.1.1. Will be held on the first Tuesday of every third month. Unless otherwise communicated, they will be held at the current Moderator's home.

       4.1.2. Are for current members only. No prospective member may attend a business meeting.

       4.1.3. Are mandatory for all current members. Members who are unable to attend a business meeting will be debited three child hours, regardless of the reason.

       4.1.4. Meeting notes will be captured by the Moderator and emailed to the group following the conclusion of the meeting.

    4.2. Playgroups

4.2.1. Will be held on the third Saturday of each month. Unless otherwise noted, playgroups will be held at XYZ Playground.

4.2.2. Prospective members are required to attend at least one playgroup meeting, prior to seeking admittance into the coop.

4.2.3. Current members are encouraged to attend as many playgroups as possible, but are not required to attend.

4.2.4. The Moderator is the only member required to attend all playgroups. Should the Moderator be unable to attend a playgroup, it is their responsibility to find a member to replace them. This is done so as to avoid the risk that a prospective member attends a playgroup where no one else shows up.

5. FINANCES

   5.1. Members will pay an annual coop fee of $5, subject to change. This fee covers food, drink, and materials for meetings. It will be paid to the Moderator in September. Fees will be prorated from join date.

   5.2. Members will pay $20 for annual access to the coop site. This fee covers all coop scheduling, sit records, and point balances. This fee is in lieu of a coop Secretary. It will be paid directly to the coop site upon joining.

6. POINTS

6.1. Points will be tracked on the coop site, which displays a historical record of sits and balances.

6.2. Sitters will receive one point per child per hour when the sit occurs between the hours of 10 am and 8 pm.

6.3. For each hour before 10 am or after 8 pm, the sitter shall receive an additional point per hour.

6.4. For each child beyond the first, the sitter shall receive an additional half point per hour.

6.5. Time will be calculated to the nearest quarter hour. The smallest increment of points that will be awarded is 1/4. Additional time will be rounded (0 – 7 min = no credit; 8 – 14 min = ¼ point).

6.6. Time will begin once the sitter arrives at the requester's home / once the requester drops the children off at the sitter's home.

6.7. Time will end once the requester arrives home / arrives at the sitter's home to pick up the children.

6.8. Members will be allowed to go into debt up to 50 points. Members will be required to reduce their debt below 50 points before they may request a sitter.

6.9. Should a member quit the coop with a debt, he/she will be required to pay the coop $1 for each point owed.

6.10. Members who have not participated in the coop for 12 months or more will be considered to have quit. At that time, debt repayment will be due.

7. REQUESTER RULES

   7.1. All sit requests must be created on the coop site.

   7.2. It is the sole discretion of the requester to select a sitter from those members that offer. Once the requester has selected a sitter, he/she will confirm the sitter as soon as possible via the coop site.

   7.3. The requester may cancel sits up until the day before, penalty-free. If the requester cancels a sit the day of the sit, he/she must pay the sitter half the expected points to compensate for the inconvenience.

   7.4. Unless otherwise agreed upon, it is the requester's responsibility to provide food, diapers, and any other necessities for the children during the sit.

   7.5. The requester must phone the sitter if he/she is to be more than 15 minutes late.

   7.6. Unless otherwise communicated explicitly to the sitter, no one other than the requester or the other parent may pick up the children.

   7.7. It is the sitter's responsibility to confirm the points for the sit and modify, if necessary, before transferring payment to the sitter.

8. SITTER RULES

8.1. The sitter must communicate to and receive approval from the requester if there is anyone other than the sitter's immediate family to be present during the sit.

8.2. The sitter may cancel up until the day before, penalty-free. If the sitter cancels a sit the day of the sit, he/she must pay the requester half the expected points to compensate for the inconvenience.

8.3. The sitter is not to transport the children to or from the sit location, unless explicitly agreed upon with the requester.

8.4. The sitter is never to inflict corporal punishment on any child in his/her care.

8.5. The sitter may not release the children to anyone other than the requester, unless explicitly agreed upon prior.

9. DISPUTE RESOLUTION

    9.1. Members must attempt to resolve disputes between themselves before contacting the Moderator.

    9.2. If members cannot reach resolution, they may ask the Moderator to intervene.

    9.3. The Moderator can credit and debit members as needed.

    9.4. The Moderator must listen to each member's story before making a decision.

9.5. The Moderator's decision is to be respected as final.

Medical Authorization Form

I, _____ Parent / Guardian of _____ do hereby give my consent to _____ {Coop Name Here}____, to secure and authorize such emergency medical treatment as the above name might require while under the supervision of said care provider. I also agree to pay all the costs and fees contingent on emergency medical care or treatment for this person as secured or authorized under this consent.

NOTE: Every effort will be made to notify the parents/ son/ daughter/ guardian, etc. in case of an emergency.
In the event of an emergency, it would be necessary to have the following information:

Physician Name: _____

Phone Number: _____

Preferred Hospital:_____

Address: _____

Phone: _____

If the parents/guardian is unavailable, other relatives or persons to contact in emergency:

Name:_____

Address:_____

Phone: _____

Relationship: _____

Signature of parents/ guardian:
_____

Date: _____

Home Safety Checklist

The following is an extremely thorough home safety checklist that may be used during a Home Visit evaluation. You may tear these pages out and copy them for use. (For the most up-to-date checklist, please visit http://kidshealth.org.)

Kitchen	Yes / No
Are knives, forks, scissors, and other sharp tools in a drawer with a childproof latch?	
Have you installed a dishwasher lock so kids can't reach breakable dishes, knives, and other dangerous objects?	
Have you installed a stove lock and have knob protectors been placed on the stove knobs?	
Are chairs and stepstools positioned away from the stove?	
When cooking, are all pot handles on the stove turned inward or placed on back burners where your child can't reach them?	
Are glass objects and appliances with sharp blades stored out of reach?	
Is the garbage can behind a cabinet door with a childproof latch?	
Are all appliances unplugged when not in use, with cords out of reach?	
Are all vitamin or medicine bottles stored in a high	

cabinet far from reach?	
Are matches and lighters stored in a locked cabinet?	
Is the cabinet under the sink free of cleaning supplies, bug sprays, dishwasher detergent, and dishwashing liquids? And are these supplies out of the reach of children?	
Are any bottles containing alcohol stored out of reach?	
Are all plastic garbage bags and sandwich bags out of reach?	
Are any cords or wires from wall telephones out of reach?	
Are refrigerator magnets and other small objects out of reach?	
Are childproof latches installed on all cabinet doors?	
Is there a working fire extinguisher?	
Does the child's highchair have a safety belt with a strap between the legs?	

Bedroom	Yes / No
Does the changing table have a safety belt?	
Are all painted cribs, bassinets, and high chairs made after 1978? (Prior to this, paint was lead based.)	
Is the crib mattress firm and flat? Does it fit snugly in the crib?	
Are window blind and curtain cords tied with clothespins or specially designed cord clips? Are they kept well out of reach and away from cribs?	
Are dressers secured to walls with drawers closed?	
Do the lids on toy chests or toy storage containers have a	

lid support to keep them from slamming shut? Are all toy chests non-locking?	
Has a window guard been placed on any window that isn't an emergency exit?	
Are any night-lights in the room not touching any fabric like bedspreads or curtains?	

Doors, Windows, Floors, and Stairs	Yes / No
Are walls in good condition, with no peeling or cracking paint (which could contain lead in older homes)?	
Are rugs secured to floors or fitted with anti-slip pads underneath?	
Have you installed a finger pinch guard on doors?	
Have you removed the rubber tips from all door stops or installed one-piece door stops?	
Have you placed doorknob covers on doors so that your toddler won't be able to leave the house?	
Do all glass doors in the house contain decorative markers so they won't be mistaken for open doors?	
Do all sliding doors have childproof locks?	
Are there safety bars or window guards installed on upper-story windows?	
Are window blind cords tied with clothespins or specially designed cord clips?	
Are bookshelves and other furniture secured with wall brackets so they can't be tipped over?	
Is there protective padding on any corners of coffee tables, furniture, and countertops that have sharp edges?	

Have you checked that all used or hand-me-down baby equipment hasn't been recalled?	
Are there hardware-mounted safety gates at the top and bottom of every stairway?	
Are stairways clear of tripping hazards, such as loose carpeting or toys?	
Have you placed a guard on banisters and railings if your child can fit through the rails?	
Are the railings and banisters secured?	
Is the door to the basement steps kept locked?	

Electrical and Heating / Cooling	Yes / No
Are all unused outlets covered with safety plugs?	
Are all major electrical appliances grounded?	
Have cord holders been used to keep longer cords fastened against walls?	
Have you checked for and removed other potential electrical fire hazards, such as overloaded electrical sockets and electrical wires running under carpets?	
Are televisions, computers, and stereo equipment positioned against walls?	
Are all radiators and baseboard heaters covered with childproof screens if necessary?	
Have gas fireplaces been secured with a value cover or key?	
Do all working fireplaces have a screen and other barriers in place when in use?	
Have you placed a list of emergency phone numbers near	

each phone in your home?	
Are there fire extinguishers installed on every floor and in the kitchen?	
Are there smoke detectors on each floor of your home?	
Have smoke detectors been installed in the hallways between all bedrooms of your home?	
Have you tested all smoke detectors within the last month?	
If you cook with or heat your home with natural gas or have an attached garage, have you considered installing a carbon monoxide detector in your home?	

Bathroom, Laundry, and Garbage	Yes / No
Is the thermostat on the hot water heater set below 120° F (49° C)?	
Are razor blades, nail scissors, and other sharp tools stored in a locked cabinet?	
Are childproof latches installed on all drawers and cabinets?	
Do the outlets have grounded fault circuit interrupters (which protect against electrocution if an electrical appliance gets wet)? (If you live in an older home that may not be "up to code," have an electrician inspect your circuit breaker panel.)	
Are toilets always left closed? Is there a toilet-lid lock on the toilet?	
Are all hair dryers, curling irons, and electric razors unplugged when not in use?	
Are there nonskid strips on the bottoms of bathtubs?	

Are there nonslip pads under rugs to hold them securely to the floor?	
Are all prescription and nonprescription medications, cosmetics, and cleaners stored in a locked cabinet? Are childproof caps on all medications?	
Are all tools and supplies used for gardening, automotive, and lawn care stored safely away from children?	
Are all hazardous automotive, pool, and gardening products in a locked area?	
Are recycling containers storing glass and metal out of reach? Are garbage cans covered?	
Are all bleaches, detergents, and any other cleaning products out of reach?	
Are laundry chutes locked with childproof locks?	

About the Author

Erica Zidel is a mother of one who is passionate about discovering ways to live a simpler, more fulfilling, and more connected life. She is the founder of the babysitting coop management site, SittingAround (www.sittingaround.com). Erica holds a bachelor's degree from Harvard, and lives with her family in Boston.

www.ingramcontent.com/pod-product-compliance
Lightning Source LLC
Chambersburg PA
CBHW071730040426
42446CB00011B/2305